The Art of Salvage

The Art of Salvage

poems by
Bill Morgan

Bill Morgan
4-13-16

DOWNSTATE
LEGACIES
Normal, Illinois

DOWNSTATE LEGACIES

Published by Downstate Legacies
Illinois State University
4241 Publications Unit
Normal, Illinois 61790-4241
http://english.illinoisstate.edu/pubunit/

Copyright © 2016 by Bill Morgan
All Rights Reserved
Manufactured in the United States of America

Distributed to the trade by Small Press Distribution
1341 Seventh Street, Berkeley, CA 94710
www.spdbooks.org

Cover and Book Design: Publications Unit, Department of English, Illinois State University, Director: Steve Halle; Production Assistant: Tess Ward; University High School Apprentices: Sydni Ritsema, Isabel Dawson, LeeAnn Broderick, Anastasia Ervin, Elizabeth Lemieux; University High School Faculty Advisor: Cassandra Graham

Cover Art: "Aquifer" (Detail) © Lisa Lofgren

ISBN 978-0-9974041-0-4
First Edition

This book was produced by the Publications Unit Partners Program at Illinois State University, in partnership with students and faculty in the Creative Writing and Publishing Club at University High School in Normal, IL. For more information, visit http://english.illinoisstate.edu/pubunit/PartnerProgram. The Partners Program has been supported by a Teaching-Learning Innovations Grant from the Center for Teaching, Learning, and Technology (CTLT) at Illinois State University.

Contents

Prologue: Certificate of Origin	1

I

Morning Pause	5
Body Language	6
The Mortal Frame	7
Self-Portrait: Nature Film	8
September Coming On	9
Reckoning: Autumn Afternoon	10
Carnal Knowledge	11
Waking to Absence	13
Elegy	14
The Widower Poems	
1. Widower at a Weddimg	15
2. Widower with Sunflowers	16
3. Widower Receives a Visitor	17
4. Widower in Wintertime	18
5. Widower Plants a Garden	19
Among the Family Photos	20
Father's War Diary	22
What the Old Poet Said	23
Slipping Into Silence	25
Losing Ground	26

II

Looking Down	29
These Slender Green Worlds	30
Six Tree Sparrows	32
Three Surprises	33
Tribute	34
Turn About	35

Body and Breath	36
Ephemeroptera	37
The Pale Persistence	38
Equinox	39
Town Crows at Winter Nightfall	40
A Flight of Nouns	
1. Murmuration	42
2. Murder	43
3. Parliament	44
4. Kettle	45
5. Exaltation	46
Among Goldfinches	47

III

Christmas Morning	51
Furnace Repair	52
Just Right	53
Herding Instinct	54
Holdout	55
Restoration	56
Spirits of the Field	58
Country Manners: Harvest	59
Of Earth and Air	
1. Gravitas	61
2. Levitas	62
Mud Shoes	63
Dorset Summer: Two Postcards Home	64
Lammas Moon	65
A Second Eden	67
Epilogue: My Father's Cigarettes	68
Notes and Acknowledgments	69
About the Poet	70

for Ellen

Prologue: Certificate of Origin

That beginning
of which we speak,
emergence into being
seen and named

                    August 19, 1940, 11:10 PM, it says
                    here on this brown document

the moment of separation

                    after 6 1/2 hours of labor

from the maternal body

                    the mother—white, housewife, age 25

not the systole-diastole,
scatter-return of pulsing
anonymous cells
mixing a human potion *in utero*
from two batches of DNA

                    the father—white,
                    service station manager, age 27

still less the ancestral grit
from upstream creeks—four-
then eight-fold, and so on back—
swept down in diffuse narrative
lines to that time and place

                    Crawford W. Long Hospital,
                    Atlanta, where Doctor M. P.
                    Pentecost, and L. Thornton, RN
                    anesthetized the woman and hovered
                    near until she had brought forth a son,
                    whose eyes they treated with 1%
                    silver nitrate solution, lest the mother
                    be a carrier of gonorrhea
                    and unwittingly blind her child

and not at all
the ambient air
and foundational earth,
the intimate gravity
of the local, the weight of distant
events bearing down
                                      on that hot Georgia red clay August night,
                                      the wooden blades of overhead fans
                                      humming through the humid air,
                                      anesthesia and sightlessness
                                      soaking the half-lit room

having flooded already across Berlin,
Paris, London, into Auschwitz—
even into Mexico, where next day
one Ramón Mercader, a Soviet agent,
would take up an ice-axe and calmly
split open Leon Trotsky's head.

I

I saw a grey-haired man, a figure of hale age, sitting at a desk and writing.

—H. G. Wells

Morning Pause

She silences the cruel clock,
sighs, turns lazily onto her side
and reaches across to cup his warm
skin-pouch—soft nest for the two small eggs
inside—against her palm. He stirs;
she kisses him on the shoulder.
                                    Their minds
are climbing like mist into the light;
their indolent bodies are sinking, heavy
and still in love with sleep.
                            He replies
in mirror-form, his hand resting
lightly along the low hills and central
valley of the *mons veneris*—warm too,
rising-falling on slowing waves
of breath.
              Soon the familiar touch
of the long-partnered, settled pair
has done its work: all their cells
are realigned, reset and ready
to lift them up to tidy the covers
and join the day, already in progress.

Body Language

My old knees are ravenous,
so I feed them Tylenol.

Pain is another hunger—
the body clamoring for something
to still it, to harmonize
its processes with time,
within whose laws it lives
in chronic antagonism
until the two have merged.

For now, I stretch, massage, and medicate—
and contemplate that other ache, desire.

The Mortal Frame

This morning the body hangs
loosely, pinned at the shoulders,
like a wet costume in the shape
of muscles, guts, and bones;
eye sockets pucker and sag;
left knee, right index finger
pop and crack their warnings:
Don't expect too much.

But how much? Aged for years,
what manner of fleshly apparatus,
what human device is this I inhabit?
Seasoned, sound, and broken in,
or rusty rattly antique?

The evidence equivocates:
summer weather, two weeks
of weights and cycling, would iron
and fluff it out or (pick
your metaphor) wax
and tune it up again;

but this gray morning it hangs
there negotiating with time
and gravity, aches a little,
reminds me it's headed down
not up—while it teases, playful
and arbitrary, grinning with
upstanding self-contradiction.

Self-Portrait: Nature Film

Out of the quiet cave,
blinking in the light,
yawning, sniffing the air
licking his lips,
testing his limbs,
idly rubbing his butt
on a nearby tree—
rested, curious,
content

until the first
taste of berries

pulls him lurching
happily ahead, nose down,
snuffling in deep
fresh grass, flanks
caressed, combed
by early season
brush and briars—
tracking the body's memory,
following the bright river.

September Coming On

Harder to find the shiny-black ones among the wild cherries, now mostly wrinkled and purple-gray, dotting the tree-lined edge of the bicycle trail. (And somebody keeps on turning up the volume in the right ear—*face it: you're running out of chances.* Left one steady—*live as if the body's appetites and joys are yours forever; anything else, you're dead already.*) These few small, wild fruits are autumn-plump, firm—and sweet as peaches steeped in wine.

Reckoning: Autumn Afternoon

The year's past equinox, equipoise—
assertion still wells up in spasms,
but ending pulls like gravity tugging
at aging flesh.

Worker yellow-jackets are a menace—
desperate, bold; cast out from the hive
and doomed to late-season freelancing,
they prowl in pop cans, burrow
into small carrion on city streets
and sidewalks.

Indoor spiders wait quietly, tucked
back into corners, hardly moving
when challenged.
                       That sluggish fly,
banging against the window,
will lie brittle, light as air,
on the sill tomorrow.

At the end of the garden path,
the season's last mosquito
clings to the underside
of a lilac leaf in the late
October wind;
when I brush
against the branch, he careens off
downward, tumbling wildly to earth,
and disappears into leafmold and twigs.

Something dreadful—slow and sure—
is stalking this clear sunlight.

Carnal Knowledge

The surgeon's knife has been at us both—
claiming me long down the belly,
jogging right
around the navel,
lifting to make an isolated cut
on the left where the colostomy
hung for a while;
marking you in rows I haven't seen
across your back, again on the buttocks
and down the arm—
invading, repairing, restoring.

You were attacked from without,
a terrible scream of speeding metal—
they lifted away
the skin of your back
to save a peeled left arm;
I from within—a part of me
tried to die and nearly poisoned the rest.

But someone skillful
visited our bodies with instruments,
and left us alive
with a make-do wholeness—
flesh stretched open, drawn tight again
in articulate lines, zones of pink:
"Careful; I was broken here."

When we open to each other,
my flesh history is written plain—
here, run your finger down the line

and read; yours, though, is behind, as if
irrelevant: know me frontally—now;
forget the rest, you seem to say, deftly
removing your shirt and lying back in the dark.

I comply, tender, happy as a child—
hands, lips, chest touching you—carnal
without knowledge.
                          For trying to know
the body unmarked is vain; the beauty
of wholeness—like your perfect belly—
compels but doesn't signify; it speaks
transcendence, lands me somewhere outside
where history, the only witness, falls silent.

I crave love's anchor, the particular:
come, turn around; let me touch your scars
and read. I know their language already.

Waking to Absence
(for a friend—a fellow-poet and a breast cancer survivor)

Mine are the usual diminishments—
   forest of hair that defeated
   clippers, comb, and brush
   now a polished clear-cut;
   tight, rippled chest and belly
   now slipping down on gravity's
   stubborn, earthward insistence.

But yours is of another order—
   intimate, absolute—
   blunt healing work
   of anesthetics, knives—
   you waking to absence
   where the armpits open
   like mouths, yawning.

No, no special grief, you say
   to my surprise: *all loss*
   is but violence diffused,
   slowed down, made tolerable
   by the eye of irony's dry
   affection, naturalized
   by imagination's alchemy.

Elegy

Because in your soul's house—
your speech—
joy is shut away
in closets
beyond your tongue or my inquiry,
we two cannot bend back time,
recover conversation's compact pleasures
or bid love hail and heal us, dear
mistress of sorrow,
who is not lost, perhaps,
except to me,

who would fold away your grief,
store it in rows—or eat it—
if that would lift it from you,
give you back that terraced voice,

intimate, small, elegant as your shoulders,
intonations as of violets
if they could speak, and playful
as the wind setting an oak leaf
upright on the fence outside
our kitchen window
that afternoon
while we watched.

The Widower Poems

1. Widower at a Wedding

In the welcome half-dark
he knocks back champagne,
twists knots in his napkin,
curses her: *damn you*!

The nuptial speeches
are eloquent, tender;
he loves the bright bride
and groom, their courage:
She has transformed my life. . . .
He is the man of my dreams. . . .
May God, or somebody,
see them safely through.

His chest, breath, voice
catch at young joy,
vein it with loss—
and again: *damn you*!

2. Widower with Sunflowers

The light tap of seeds falling onto an earthenware plate—
bink-bink. He's in the afternoon kitchen, stripping them
from the hard, brown heads of late-season wild sunflowers.

Blossom-face down, twisting counter-clockwise,
thumbs against the back, index and middle fingers
beneath, fanning the snug little casings as they pass:

*Bink; bink-bink, bink.   You should be here with me;
this is the work we did together: gathering ripeness
for a future radiance we could imagine.   Bink-bink.*

He takes one onto his thumb, eats it: the crisp, piney taste.
His hands are lightly oiled, sticky; he sniffs the sharp,
clean, penetrating smell: turpentine and basil.

He's working this gray October morning for the spring to come,
planning a brilliant summer larder for the delicate goldfinches
who will bury their hungry faces in the new season's yellow suns.

*If you were here, I would nuzzle your fingers and offer you mine.
You have taken yourself away—elsewhere; it is your right to do that.
But you cannot take away the autumn, sunflowers, goldfinches—
my harvest of year's-end fullness for a springtime we should have shared.*

3. Widower Receives a Visitor

In his dream, she sat behind him,
still, in the deer blind all afternoon;
then back at the house at dusk,

she stretched out under the quilt
his sister had made and lay
reading his father's diary.

After chili, cheese, and pears,
they walked the block; he stroked
the neighbors' cats; she watched.

When nine arrived, she waved
from her shiny black car
as it pushed a hole in the dark.

4. Widower in Wintertime

As if a tape were rewound,
she slips back into his life—
bundled in the oak rocker, reading,
or silhouetted in the passenger seat
against the snowy countryside.

Her image flickers—bodiless
and without a track to the future.
Arms that would reach out hang useless,
and the calendar reels ahead,
a cold and lightless tunnel.

What is this approximation,
soft-focus imitation that projects
itself against a chilly day
stranded outside flesh and time?

Why do you come here?

5. Widower Plants a Garden

Spinach, arugula, six tomatoes,
four peppers, three rows of okra,
three of runner beans:

this wholesome future, projected
abundance, laid in beside
asparagus and strawberries she knew.

He will eat it all. Or what
he can't, he'll can or freeze
against the leaner times.

Among the Family Photos

In the dresser mirror,
a gaunt and graying man
is winding my grandfather's
Elgin pocket watch;
sixteen turns, then he sets it back
among the family photos.

Over here the faces look out at me—
mother, father, two sons, and
the mirror-man, who sets me thinking
about lineage—his finger
and thumb humming a rhythmic,
secular prayer to the gods
of genetic continuity.
Some insinuating comfort
curls inside a tale of origins.

But this one's a broken fable,
a confusing heap of springs and wheels:
Grandpa died when Daddy was sixteen;
nobody living knows when he
got the watch, how long he owned it,
if he used it every day,
if it mattered to him. Years after
he laid it down for the last time,
Daddy had it recased in well-
intentioned 50's stainless steel,
thinking the gold plate worn
unattractively thin.

When Daddy died,
it came to me, looking bright

but pulseless and uncomfortable
in its silvery metallic lab coat.

Now it's repaired, restored
in flea-market gold plate
of the right time and style,
but with someone else's initials
on the back. I must have them replaced
with WLM, so this mute relic
of William Leonard Morgan, blacksmith
can tell without contradiction
the story I'm listening for.

This is your grandfather's watch,
the mirror-man says, and I can see a twenty-year old
stepping out into Atlanta summer
after service at the Baptist Church,
lifting it out of his waistcoat pocket,
thinking of Lessie Flynn
and Sunday dinner; or, a few years on,
hauling it up from his leather apron,
wiping his face, laying down the hammer
and heading into the house for lunch;
or later still, pacing, checking
the time, straining for the cry
from the next room;
or in his nightshirt, chilly
in the last glow of the coal fire,
turning this stem every night,
storing up tensile strength,
expecting a tomorrow.

Father's War Diary: 1945

How hard to love a man
who writes of Japs and queers
and treats the drunken riots
of Frisco liberty with his sailor pals
as a kind of sport: *The room's
a wreck. Somebody has bought
a bed, I think. Total liquor
consumed 7 qts; beer 8 gallons...*

How hard to blame a man,
young wife and babies—*sweetest
gal...my boy...little princess*—
at home while he's up to his nose
in an ocean of snipers, ships, planes,
torpedoes—all trying to kill him:
I've never in my life been so afraid—
skipper and officers he resents,
sweat, bad food, and alien names:
Iwo Jima, Eniwetok, Hilo,
Lingayen Gulf, and Nagasaki.

How hard to pull him close
or push him away, to find
the angle, stance, distance to free
my yearning to know and claim him
whose little book is like a gnarly
cactus, dotted with blossoms: *The odor
just blew by for dinner—fish...
His body, what was left of it,
disappeared into the smoke and fog
and drifted out to sea.*

What the Old Poet Said

I shouldn't answer, really.
I'll embarrass you—or myself.
But, OK: the short answer is
I wish I had had more sex.

Are you shocked? No? Shall I go on?
Very well. You asked; I'll tell you.

   I loved that fresh, open bodily
   joy—new every time—passed
   back and forth with mouths, lips,
   and tongues—a shapely narrative
   of breath and skin taking them
   into the cave of pleasure and back out,
   the senses making their own poems and stories.

   It was like a story, you know—or maybe
   more like a symphony, in movements:
   first the tongue and lips in happy
   curiosity sample the textures—
   the animal motions of the mouth
   holding and tasting the special
   other-skin of the other.

Then the sweet, sympathetic pleasure
of nurturing a partner's slow-sure climb—
listening for the breaths, jagged, even,
and deep, following the track up
and down the slopes, staying close,
feeling the nerve endings stretching—
reaching, reaching for more and more.

Then the wish—deep and strong—
to take the other's pleasure into yourself
as it mounts, strong and salty
like the waves and waters of the sea;
breath and movement matching
the other up to a helpless peak
and down the bumpy slopes into
quiet, open contentment.

And there, at that place, the near
joining of two people's flesh,
holding close to your body's
welcome joy as I wait here
just outside it. I will be still
and hold you carefully
while you breathe out the last
ripples and let your limbs go slack.

Well, that's enough of that.
More than you wanted, I'll wager.
Are you embarrassed? Disgusted?

I may come to wish
I hadn't said so much…

But I can't regret that shivering pleasure.

Now close that shade, please—
then go; I want to sleep.

Slipping Into Silence

He has loved the warm touch of this noisy world,
where now a glacier is rising around him.

The huge roar of life, like sunlight's gift,
has dimmed to a pale and distant flute.

His beloved's words are polished stones
laid one against the other in a stream—

no crisp, dry edges to hold them apart
and allow them space to open into meaning.

Lifelong he has loved the noisy-bright world!
This quiet grief is the price he must pay.

Losing Ground

Following the diagnosis
and all the expert advice,

he set about regrading the landscape
to turn the waves away.

He installed shunts and drains
to give the floods back to the tide.

He raised the seawall another foot.

Good. Enjoy it now, they said.

> He will. But nothing avails
> forever, he knows: the blind
> waters will have their way.

II

Consider all this; and then turn to the green, gentle, and most docile earth, both the sea and the land; and do you not find a strange analogy to something in yourself?

—Herman Melville

Looking Down

From above like this, square miles are real things. Scores of them, green tiles, pass under the belly of the plane as it makes its way up the length of Illinois. Each block is uniquely itself, but the materials repeat and repeat—farmhouse, outbuildings, corn and beans—human work snugged up against a ditch, a river, a patch of woodland—and all contained by roads that mark century-and-a-half-old grid imposed upon the faceless prairie. That grid is the lattice within whose lines settlers and heirs have stitched the quilts of their lives.

These Slender Green Worlds

A line of timber breaking the tailored cropland
signals a river dropping slowly downward,
slipping toward the larger stream. That gray-
green stripe shadows a sunken, wilder place,
where farm fields disappear behind the banks,
where the current pulls a canoe into a sun-
flecked tunnel of oaks and maples leaning across
the channel, pale roots grasping at air. The heron
lifts away, the doe stiffens, then turns
to climb the bank. The Plymouth chassis hunkers
at the flood plain's edge, and the kingfisher studies minnows
from the wringer washer half-buried in sandy shallows.

Sparer, shorter growth means a railroad bed,
abandoned to tires and ashes, to creosote rafters
for the woodchuck's den—or a fence row laced with wire
and rotting posts, mulberry thickets and thorny
locusts shading a web of paths that the skunk
and possum follow from field and hedge to ditch
and road. The redbuds and willows are crowded back
onto a couch and roofing shingles; a poplar
peers out here and there at ranks of advancing
houses; the cherry and sumac make a stand
against the concrete and plow, and the feral rose—
blazing yellow through a rusted bedspring—
guards the cardinal's eggs and the rabbit's young.

These slender worlds of green, these filaments
of wildness laid across the straining land,
swallow our oversights, embrace what we

neglect, discard, or fail to dominate
and wait—in lines luxuriant with life—

for wisdom or exhaustion to prevail
and shift this burden, lift this death they bear.

Six Tree Sparrows

Among the dozens of Juncos, six Tree Sparrows
low in the snow-crusted field, make their way westward
through mixed grasses, repeating a low, contented
harvest song, calling discreetly to one another
in calm, candid voices like so many small wooden flutes.

In this late-afternoon work, each bird settles
about two feet up on a pale yellow Foxtail
seed spike, slim and tall, and rides it down—
tail and wings buzzing in quick bursts, for balance—
then slides along toward the brown tip,
pins the cluster to the ice and strips it, telling and re-telling
a narrative of progress to the others, who listen,
feed, and reply. This goes on, stem after stem, for half an hour;
it is a labor elegant, precise, so perfectly fitted to itself
that one watching could almost believe in a peaceable god.

Then their little rusty caps, black breast spots, and white-
barred wings rise and disappear into darkening trees behind.

Three Surprises

Under his morning coat,
felt cap and gray trousers,
the catbird sports a flashy,
rose-scarlet thong.

The beaver's bristled lip,
black and wet, slides over
pumpkin-orange teeth.

At the deep center point
in the mounded white
of the Queen Anne's Lace,
I find a single blood-red petal.

Tribute

All right then, a dandelion
sometimes—jaunty
chuckling rogue.

A shifter too—say,
a mayapple—covering
the naked white blossom
with green leaf and bole.

But always
an iris—

proud, timid
private, open.

Turn About
(Clyffe Farm, Dorset)

A mile down the road, a falconer
watches sharply, now and then
releasing his black-eyed, efficient bird,
a Saker, to take a Wood Pigeon off
the glistening watercress beds and bring
the limp carcass back.

Here next to my window, the combine
creeps around the field while Buzzards
perch or hover, then suddenly drop:
a panicked mouse, confused and scrambling
at the vertical edge of standing wheat,
transforms to fur and flesh.

Body and Breath

Six warm days, he held his rib cage taut—
muscles firm and intact, face impassive,
hair shining back at the morning sun.

On the chilly seventh, his chest dropped,
his fur bleached to gray; only the mask
and ringed tail left to say *raccoon*.

He exhaled a rank corruption
that followed my bike for fifty yards
along the growling road that broke him.

I pedaled hard, contemplating his life,
my kind—sucking in, pushing out
the heavy, raw, saw-toothed air.

Ephemeroptera

Creatures of this order,
the filmy mayflies,
break the membrane, shake off the water, and rise
for their mating—an airborne quickie—
then fall back to drop their eggs and die,
all in less than a day.

A dedicated life—focused,
narrow even—it may seem to us,
who name them thus;

as we—frail, fluttering—must seem
to stabler things—say, rocky shale,
limestone, marble, granite—which,
themselves, in the eye of time
are brief as desire

and shapeless as the dust
within them
they are becoming.

The Pale Persistence

Now is the yellow season
shading into orange-brown
of goldenrod and sunflower—
and after this, the white.

April's snowy bloodroot, trillium,
spilled into the pink and blue
of soapwort, vetch, and chicory;
but summer-long, the ghostly sheen
of cherry, locust, blackberry—
the pale insistence sounding through
the greening leaf and reddening fruit:
the pedal-bass of blossom white.

Clouds of wild asters now—the time
of bronzing corn and caterpillars
liveried in black and rust—
they bend and brush the earth,
and warn: *after this the white.*
Yes. After this, the white.

Equinox

The timid sun is poised
for its scripted, slow return

to dominance, a trek
that will tame the night, releasing

muscles and breath I've held
in wire-tight strapping, unable

to risk a full exhale
through months of heavy dark.

These warm arcs of radiant
clear sky invite release

and mask for now the cooler,
darker side of moon

and sun to which, chastened,
I know I must return

when warmth has done its half-year's
work and ice flows in again.

Town Crows at Winter Nightfall

At the corner by the church, I pause
in my walk to watch them arrive
again tonight—two hundred
or more black, noisy outlines
spilling out where three trees
slice upward into the steely
belly of a winter sky. I smile,
enjoy their motion and prattle,
as they settle in—these odd,
new neighbors—self-involved,
muttering, leaning into the bitter
wind, getting on with the business
of being town crows at winter
nightfall.   They fringe the tops
of the trees like ill-fitting caps—
slippery berets—now jaunty,
now severe; they jostle each other,
careen off in little bursts
of flight, then re-alight upwind,
shoulders and voices haggling
over the six-inch interval their kind
require of proper lodging.

They are *other, not me*, I remind
myself, and for this—their wildness,
indifference—I value them, making
my way home—the world re-centered—
in the fading light.

               But later,
a drowsy imagination—spring-loaded,

imperiously human—claims them:
shows me well-dressed bird shapes,
workers dispersing in a misty
dawn—to desk jobs, factories,
farms, schools, and highway crews—
then gathering again come evening
at The Maple Trees boarding house
to talk over the day, complain,
abuse the weather, bargain,
then sleep like the rest of us.

A Flight of Nouns

1. Murmuration

The restless starlings, a flowing
company of hundreds, home in
on the tall reeds at dusk:
they move against the sky
as a whisper might drift
on wind, as a patch of oil
rides the surface of a creek.

The mass of them stretches,
folds into a moving center,
compressing and scattering—

now a wisp of smoke,
now a black tornado,
now a dark mound of dough
wildly kneading itself—

as each agile black dot
seeks the cluster's midpoint,
away from the vulnerable edge
where predators do their work.

2. Murder

I wouldn't put it past them—
quick, resourceful, cocky—
gangs of them driving squirrels
and sparrows off feeders,
dive-bombing owls and hawks.

And then there's the one in my birch
last winter…Like a hungry raptor,
he swept in, picked up a starling
with his feet, pinned it to a branch
and hammered hard at the sternum,
pausing to check his surroundings,
then pounding again, until the small
wings slowed and stopped.

The others stood by and cheered
as he stripped the red breast meat
and let the black remnants fall
onto soft, oblivious snow.

3. Parliament

In flocks, they'd be impressive—formal in manner and looking dignified in gray-brown tweed and big, rimmed spectacles. Numbers would magnify their *gravitas*. They can turn their heads on the fluffy post of a short, thick neck so as to see almost the whole horizon without shifting their feet. *Circumspection*.

I'm starting to see it: Screech Owls, Horned, Barred, Spotted, Long-eared, Short-eared, Burrowing, Saw-Whet, Snowy, and Barn, all clamoring, "Mr. Speaker, Mr. Speaker," then, at the gavel, slipping into their desks as if scattering to the branches of an oak where they sit, blink, listen, and ponder in the solemn, half-dark as laws, like sausages, are improvised by those trusted to act with *wisdom*.

Still, such grave attributions can be no comfort to the mouse in the corn stubble, when the swift and deadly shadow washes over him.

4. Kettle

Swainson's and Broad-wings,
hundreds of them loafing up there,
rising and turning like bubbles
in thermal waves of water,
their silhouettes lifted and contained
by tall columns of wind, not iron,
enamel, copper, or stainless steel.

This is no casual gathering: they ride
the heated air, round and round,
clockwise and counter, tending
always southward in a leisurely, indirect
progress—their patient migration.

Songbirds, ducks and geese, even
other hawks like the Sharp-shinned,
barrel straight toward Mexico and beyond,
but these confident, unhurried ones
circle and hold formation. This slow
simmer will get them there—they'll be
done in due course, in plenty of time.

5. Exaltation

What looks like joy to us,
when they circle upward
singing all the way to the top,
sometimes a thousand feet in the air,
is the workaday smack-talk
of the male declaring his ground.

What looks and sounds like
choral and balletic cooperation,
when they appear in diffuse groups,
rise, hover, and sing, then rise again,
drop from that great height,
rise again and sing, as if greeting
one another, is territorial bragging
and ritualized warning: *keep out.*

The ladies like it, apparently.
They slip in and pick a fella,
and quickly then, the ecstasy
turns earthward, becomes the daily work
of nesting, incubating, feeding—
though he still slips out and up
from time to time, to check out the place,
hum a little from way up there.

He knows the melody by heart.

Among Goldfinches

I am floating in a thin cloud
of them—simultaneous with
their soft whistles and rhythmic,
undulating flight—their tiny bodies
suspended just next to my ears
and shoulders, as we inhabit
each other's space and speed
and direction for a dozen wingbeats
and easy pedal strokes,
coasting on the morning wind.

Then they bank off, settle,
and sit like bright blossoms
in scrubby trailside locusts, watching
my ordinary bicycle plunge ahead
into a canyon of Queen Anne's lace.

Later, as I struggle home against
the wind, their ghosts are glazing
my arms like dew and wrapping
the street full of traffic and starlings
in a yellow nimbus, dropping
an airy twitter and flutter of wings
onto the rolling earth, then drifting off
with a shy glance—feathered spirits
teasing like a voice that whispers:
Some riders here still believe in angels.

III

A man may look for gold without assuming that there is gold everywhere; if he finds gold, well and good, if he doesn't he's had bad luck.

—Bertrand Russell

Christmas Morning

Downstairs to coffee, paper, a blown bulb,
and a glowing screen full of unanswered emails.

A wind-whipped cardinal picks at the empty feeder;
the neighbors' Santa flounders face down in the snow.

On the early news, zealots have bombed a church
during mass in Nigeria, killing twenty-five.

Welcome, child. Good luck. So much to be set right…

Furnace Repair

How's the patient?—I'm bending
down in the cellar to watch:
Don't know; still opening him up.

Minutes later, he's upstairs,
holding a charred igniter:
Needs a heart transplant
You have a donor?
I keep one in my truck.

You're good at this—I'm writing
the check—*this metaphor game.*
Well, the office warned me
you were a poet; I trained.

Just Right

The light is just right for a vodka tonic, I said, testing my drink, and one of the handsome men at the table laughed quietly; the other one smiled and pointed across the canal at the sun, hanging behind a cormorant on the top of a mangrove—translucent black wing feathers fanned out to dry. We're at the end of "The Boys' Week," as the family calls it, and waiting to be served our own fresh-caught snapper and grouper at a local grill by the water. Tomorrow, vacation's over—just roadmaps and airports, planes out of the Keys and back to our usual late-winter lives up North. We shouldn't have been this lucky, given our histories. But that's another poem. So I'll take it—and call it happiness—this afternoon light that bends and falls across father and sons, gracing our annual affirmation.

Herding Instinct

She makes a wide, confident sweep around the sunny perimeter, moves the guests gently eastward, toward the front, where breakfast waits. Like a Welsh collie working sheep, she knows each one and steers them easily without seeming to. On her last pass, she drifts from the kitchen off south into the study, to be sure I join the flock. I do.

On the screened porch, pancakes and berries are delicious. So's her smile.

Holdout

In March, the first timid woodchuck—
A chubby, attractive offer;
then the killdeer drawing arcs
across the April gray,
the catbirds, brown thrashers,
rushing, crowding back in:
like the barely-leafed-out trees,
they promise things green and golden.

But a cool, clear, breezy morning
among white-blossoming locusts
of early May—with goldfinches,
indigo buntings, yellowthroats,
and a sun-brightened scarlet tanager—
is enough to make me sign:
Yes, I'll take the lover's lease again—
same terms for another year.

Restoration

These slick little seeds, black-brown-
gray on my fingers, promise *rattlesnake*

master, coneflowers yellow and purple,
blue aster, compass plant, tick

*trefoil, bundleflower, partridge
pea*—some of the dozen native

forbs we're mixing with green kelp meal
in a five-gallon bucket. Another holds

fluffy grasses—*little bluestem, wild rye,
prairie dropseed, indian*—stirred into pinkish-

brown Azomite before I pour
both tubs into the bins of the Bison

seed drill harnessed behind the bright-
red, borrowed tractor. The project

today is to press these antique names,
sturdy and eloquent, back into the narrative

of this ancient, glacial soil, whose tale
for a hundred years has been spoken in corn

and beans, in *brome, timothy, fescue*—
alien tongues of a vast, agricultural epic,

one acre of which, about a sentence-
worth, we're rewriting this afternoon:

our small gift of color, lyric voice
restored to the muffled, patient earth.

Spirits of the Field

The Greeks believed they hid inside the trees,
but here in the heartland, the nymphs and dryads play—
where else?—in summer corn and soybean fields.

See?—there they are—wind-surfing the blue-green
seas of beans and, next field over, stilt-walking
between the tall, wind-washed ranks of corn.

So suited to the place they are, they might
be taken for barn swallows feeding low,
or the velvet-covered tines of white-tailed bucks.

These are the ordinary demigods of local
earth—of seed and rain, of sun and air.

Country Manners: Harvest

On local two-lanes, you meet a windshield
with a man's face in it, and odds are
he'll lift his index finger, slowly, off
the steering wheel, maybe just ten degrees—
an impassive salute. Gravity's tugging hard
in farm country this time of year; it'll pull
the beans right out of their pods if you let them
stand too long. And all the work—in trucks
and combines or by hand—is a wrestling match
with the magnet at the center of the earth:
resistance is precious, not to be squandered
on excess greeting—for neighbor or stranger.

The women, when they aren't in the fields
or driving grain to bins and buyers,
are sweeping—leaves off the sunken walk
up to the house, corn shucks from the drive—
pushing fallen matter away to one side
or the other: *Listen*, they say to the downward
tendency in things, *go drop your mess
somewhere else—over there*. They don't look up
unless they know the sound of the motor:
eye contact, an unseemly extravagance,
would interrupt their sober work,
a labor measured, grave, and diligent.

> Each night, in their long beds,
> wrapped in the musky dark,
> these men and women fall
> to flesh as rain and seed
> to weary soil, spring to fecund

heat, and harvest to winter
cold; heavy as gray stones,
they ride the sleepy tunnel
down to gravitation's core,

and come to rest there, I infer,
without waste—as kernel, leaf,
and limb come prudently to earth.

Of Earth and Air: Two Secular Homilies

1. Gravitas

For gravity is quick and sure:
it snatches heedless cups from hands
and smashes them on kitchen tiles;

it brings the sudden tree to earth
or into bedrooms in the night
to prophesy what comes at last,

when blood and nerve and sinew seize,
then shake and slip, release their portions
to blackness fell, and *all fall down.*

2. Levitas

For lightness slips the noose of grief:
it rides the paper airplane, mounting
to vision's bright blue vanishing;

it lifts the soul into the skin
when lover's touch comes summoning
and clears the body's lethargy;

it blesses bird and beast, and names
us child of thistledown and morning;
its sovereign cry is *all shall rise*.

Mud Shoes

Love is an act of imagination,
so when my lady phoned from work
to say she had jeans and mud shoes
in her car if I needed help
getting a deer out of the woods,

I recognized the genuine article

and saw her there, slim, sleek, and tidy
in classy khaki slacks with a burgundy
blouse, black phone between her shoulder
and left ear, right hand tapping a yellow
pencil on a notepad on her desk.

Dorset Summer: Two Postcards Home

1. June 15.

A tiny dry fly found me one
last-chance trout tonight—
just at dark, in a mighty wind:
the stars stood still and watched,
but everything else thrashed
about, beating the blind
and arbitrary air. I wanted you
there, whipping black night
and wrinkled water beside me.

2. August 17.

I climbed today through sunlight
so yellow you could stroke it
onto Blagdon Hill, then Bullbarrow above
the Blackmoor Vale, and White Nothe
over opal-blue-green Weymouth Bay:
the chattering gulls are in from the shore,
following the plow and gorging
on earthworms; blackberries, rich
as wine, speckle the dark hedgerows,
fall off at a touch in your hands.

All day a ghost has hung just
out of sight, whispering: this must be
what it feels like to die—to stand
on a high hill with the wind in your face
and think *How painfully beautiful
it all is.*

Lammas Moon

> We come back emptied,
> to nourish and resist
> the words of coming to rest....
> —Seamus Heaney

With others in the chattering crowd
that tumbles out into the late-night street,
I look up to see the butter-yellow,
confident moon gazing down benignly
on us: it's August 1 in Dorset—
Lammastide, feast of the early
harvest, when the Saxons broke the first
loaf at mass—with the autumn oncoming,
and we're deep in the spell of a master's poems.

The wise poet's knife-edged words—
birthplace, flagstone, byre, birthright—
and the luminous disc light my drive
home along narrow, high-hedged lanes;
they are a beacon and a talisman—

> but not for the rabbit in the white of the headlights:
> I brake to evade, but it finds the wheels—
> *whump-whump*—front and rear.

Back at the farmhouse, I park and slump
in through the dregs of a wedding party
breaking up: a young man snarls
"Then fuck it—fuck you," at a bare-shouldered girl;
they are weighted down with a sorrow older
than her small, white arms or his flushed face.

The steady light up there is now
so close I think I could touch it; still,
it looks on and offers no counsel. My neck

and shoulders are chilled; I'm hollowed out.
I want to rock shut against the graceless world.

Outside again with a glass of wine,
I lean over the wall and watch two hares
frisking in the moon-washed barley stubble.
The voice of the poet floats up, pauses
at the margin of the audible, then drifts
silently out across the meadow,
reaching toward an accord, a merger
with the large, staring Lammas moon:
faint stripes of cloud lie across the lighted
face like the last traces of a smile.

I step back in along the shining
flagstone path; I will sleep tonight
with the windows and curtains open after all.

A Second Eden
(Clyffe Farm: Dorset)

Garden tomatoes, red, rich, firm—
like eating new sunlight.

Scatters of warm, brown wheat on a granary floor—
like breathing in the morning's bread.

You gathering breakfast blackberries—
like watching time's first harvester.

River water, achingly clear—
like washing my eyes,
once and forever.

Epilogue: My Father's Cigarettes

… the dark blue pack of Montclairs next to the ashtray on the bedside table in his hospital room … i took my first one from it … we all thought he would survive the clot but he was there to die … you could smoke in hospitals in 1963 … when his ashen face with its timid embarrassed smile wasn't covered by the pale green oxygen mask we both smoked … he was fifty … i had to help him pee … he died the next day … on Father's Day … i'm not making this up … my mother sat in the hall at home in her pink nightgown lighting up and crying as she took the early morning call … we brought his things home … limp empty clothes … wallet … zippo lighter and cigarettes … i smoked them … and others until i stubbed out my last one—a Benson & Hedges—in March 1991 when i had lived three days longer than his stump of a life … a primitive animal such as a starfish he once taught me will grow a new identical limb if it loses one … its body just reaches out and inhabits the precise space left empty by the loss

Notes

Waking to Absence is a tribute to Jerry Dillon Pratt. The title comes from some lines in her poem, "So This Is."

A Flight of Nouns: Parliament: "Laws are like sausages; it is better not to see them being made."—Otto von Bismarck

A Flight of Nouns: Exaltation: The European Skylark performs a memorable song flight in which it rises slowly from the ground, fluttering constantly as if hovering. The singing continues until, after drifting around at great height, the bird suddenly stops singing and plunges back to the ground.

Acknowledgments

"Self Portrait: Nature Film" and "Carnal Knowledge" first appeared in the author's chapbook *Trackings: The Body's Memory, The Heart's Fiction* (Boulder: Dead Metaphor Press, 1998).

"Reckoning: Autumn Afternoon," "Town Crows at Winter Nightfall," "These Slender Green Worlds," "Holdout," "Among Goldfinches," "Summer: Two Postcards Home," "The Pale Persistence," and "Country Manners: Harvest" first appeared in the author's chapbook *Sky with Six Geese* (Columbus: Pudding House, 2005).

The following poems first appeared in the journals indicated:
"Certificate of Origin" in the *Sow's Ear Poetry Review*
"Body Language" and "My Father's Cigarettes" in SRPR (*Spoon River Poetry Review*).
"The Mortal Frame," "Lammas Moon," "The Widower Poems," and "Among the Family Photos" in the *Hardy Review*.
"Restoration" in *Glacial Deposits*.
"Body and Breath" in *Limestone*.

About the Poet

Bill Morgan has published two print chapbooks of poems, *Trackings: The Body's Memory, The Heart's Fiction* (Boulder: Dead Metaphor Press, 1998) and *Sky With Six Geese* (Columbus: Pudding House Press, 2005), one e-chapbook, *Spare Parts and Whole Poems in Various Shapes and Sizes* (Seventh Dream Press, 2014), as well as numbers of individual poems in journals. For many years he could be sighted in the halls, classrooms, and offices of the Department of English at Illinois State University. Under his other name, William W. Morgan, he wrote scholarly studies of Thomas Hardy. Now he is Poetry Editor for the *Hardy Review* and coproduces *Poetry Radio* for WGLT, the NPR affiliate in Normal, Illinois. He is most often seen by day in Southwest England, South Florida, or Central Illinois with a fly rod or binoculars in his hands, or with bicycle wheels under him. At night, washed over by Palestrina, Bach, Mozart, Schubert, Beethoven, Verdi, Puccini, or Barber, he hunches over a keyboard and tries to salvage poems from the detritus of the day.